Also by H. L. Raven:

Dial 999: A Jon Hunter Mystery

Razorwire Embrace

by H. L. Raven

Via Dolorosa Press
Cleveland, Ohio

Razorwire Embrace

© 2011 by H. L. Raven

Cover art and design by Elisabeth Butler

Title font "*A Font With Serifs*" by Extate

Quote from "The Lost Lie" by Anne Sexton from *45 Mercy Street* © 1976

vdp53

ISBN-10: 0-9718673-5-6
ISBN-13: 978-0-9718673-5-2

Via Dolorosa Press
701 East Schaaf Road
Cleveland, OH 44131
USA

www.viadolorosapress.com

In
honor
and
cherished memory
of
Kevin Sweet

There is rust in my mouth,
the stain of an old kiss.

- Anne Sexton

Things Fall Through The Cracks

I know this because my broken nails
led me to you, deep in the dark spot
beneath the rotted floorboards.

They say nothing could survive that long,
but survival is a difficult concept in
itself; I've been here long enough to
know that some things just don't give up
that easily. Some things really do fall
through the cracks and fester on,
waiting for the right moment to strike.

Parasite

I've got you
shoved so deep
inside of me
it would take
an exorcism
just to find
you.

I'd give my
last waking
breath for
this feeling,
let you drain
me dry til
I was just
a sack of
old bones
collecting dust
on a shelf.

There is no
difference between
love and survival.

that little black
dress I wore
just for the occasion—
a night she would
not be home,
a night I could
sin completely—

that little black
dress you tugged
off of my aching body—
making love to
me standing up
in front of
your street windows—

that little black
dress, stained with
the deep scent
of you, that
I shall never
wear again.

When You Think Of Me

I am that dream
you cry through,
that one last
waking nightmare
you refuse to
talk about.

I am what
you wish you
could kill in silence.

As Candles Die

another blink
of a coalfire eye,
four years past
the soot of creation:
I admit I was
naïve when
I took you in,
and, breathing once,
there is no lesson
I could not have
learned an easier
way, no, I
was the glowing
ember, or
maybe now the
charred darkness.

Unlike All The Other Girls

He told me I could hide
anywhere I liked,

I could count to fifty
million, throw my
voice in shadowy corners,

prostrate myself before
Christ's impaled body
and whimper the rosary,

I could memorize spells,
pretend to be invisible,
hold my breath for
four minutes under
the dark water.

He told me he
preferred it, even,

(and then the click
of a switchblade)

that it was time
for something different.

W hore

All things
come full-circle
in the end.

I found the
premise of life
on my 20th
birthday,
delivered late
but in-person,
re-gifted.

360 degrees
it presents itself.
360 degrees
with my legs
spread wide
and my breasts
in his hands.
(Oh, such putty
for a master!)

We end in
what we begin,
and he will leave
just as quickly
as he came.

R ipe

The crackle of dust
against the needle.

The scritch-scratches
from little claws
outside.

The tears when
she thinks you're
too far away to hear.

The snap of electricity
after the chain
is pulled.

The thick echo
of a strong pulse.

And You Thought You Were Being Kind

As if my eyes
were glued shut
by hope,
life colored
by what the
dream was.
Something deep
inside me wrong,
the words not
coming out
quite the way
I thought
they would.

Am I woman
or deceased?

Once, I was
what you claimed
you wanted.
Now I am
only what I was
alone.

When our lips touched,
it was more than
what you thought.

(the radiators clink
the radiators steam
the radiators need
to be bled)

That towel I cooled
your forehead with
through the fever dream
has long since been discarded,
most certainly.

Oh! But one of us does lie!

I miss such nights.
I miss such blatant sacrifice.
I miss how you would
Fuck Me Fuck Me Fuck Me.
I miss your sleep,

I miss your Sleep.

Burn

Yeah, I take
the fall.

I'm a fireworks display,
a raging constellation,
a bright streak
in the night sky.
Flames flicker at my feet
and I crackle.
The sound is a sparkler
in your ear.
I'll singe anything
that tries to catch me,
hot and smoking like
embers and ash,
because tonight,

I feel like fire.

A study in silence—

That year past,
no longer perched
at my windowsill
awaiting the familiar
sound of your footsteps.
Cracking the clock
that blinks your time,
that reminds me of anticipating
those nights filled with
the passion of lies.

Valium, Valium,
I embrace this emptiness
and know nothing of us.

You loved me once,
or so you said;
you loved our Season of Hell.

The same heat smothers me still,
only, this time,
it's not you.

If Only I Had Pushed You Over

Ragged landscape, drawn
by a rusty old plow
up mountainous stretches,
fields of prickly thumbs,
oceans of thorns, crackling
like fresh blood on a fire.

A moment not lost but
punctured, each wound
dripping instances of barren time.

It is a mirage, scrapingly arid;

Even the flowers have
given up hope, crushed
under the weight of heated breath.

Grand, indeed; tearful, of course.

Careless pebbles never touching
bottom, an unforgiving sun:

Regretting repressed anger.

Arizona

We slept all day today
like depressed patients
without medication
and I watched sullen
thoughts dance
across the bed
I did not share
with you.

You talk now about
our happy week
and I listen like
I've no recollection.
Nod yes, nod yes,
and wonder if
I'll ever know home.

Dirty Laundry

The last time I
saw you, I bit
my tongue
and pretended you
weren't still wedged
between my ribs.

Inside, the bones
were grinding.
I stood there
in my 4th death
and smiled like
it was okay
that you tossed me
aside, like I was
just asking for it.

Inside, my lungs
were ablaze, my
heart struggled
to regain control,
and my muscles
flinched, preparing
for the next blow.

Lying In Wait

He's buried in your basement
behind the box of half-burned
photographs and moldy letters.

He's covered in thorns
shaped like Christ's veins
(which were split open so you
could keep on forgetting).

He's made gouges in the
crumbling concrete walls,
gnawed on your only bible,
and left lead shavings
by the water tank.

And he knows just how long
it takes for you to
get out of your car,
unlock the door,
and turn on the lights.

Half Past Five

And I know
the churning
deep down inside
is something more
than hunger,
something beyond
the words you can
think of.

And I know
when you turn
over in bed
and think you cry
out for me,
that the alarm
clock is just
stuck.

And I know
you're sorry
about the last
nine months,
but that won't
change my
last two words.

History

R dreamt me up,
promised me the
night sky, then sat
there gazing back at
it til it faded away.

G held me down
and fucked me til
I lied, never once
asking forgiveness
or permission, his
sharpened teeth
reminding me of
what I deserved.

S taught me to
love again, turned
me into a goddess,
then disappeared to
worship the great
distance between us.

A was a mirror
that reflected all
that I loved about myself.
His loss hurt the most.

J was relieved
when I bled seas
and tried to ignore
the emptiness

in my tears.

K would have
killed me if
he got the chance,
his precious collection
clanging against the walls
each time the ground sank.

Winter

What happens when
love dies?
When the ring fades,
the glitter dulls,
and lips crease
from the drought?

It is the thought
of a bitter woman
sharing your bed
that makes me
curse the sky.
It is the memory
of my naïveté, of
my blind faith
in your confused heart,
that makes me
drive the 3rd nail in.

What happens when
love dies,
and I bury myself
with it?

New Year

Barely Monday,
your seething limbs
kept at length,
a year's winter, endless,
like your tongue tracing
the inside of my thigh:

Is this not death then?

Back arched, chilled,
a shuddering flicker;
the hours close in
as drawn as
your image,
as scratchy as
your unshaven face:

Gasping, are you not Spring?

Insomnia

3am.
You're in another town,
in the winter of the world,
where prayers fall from trees
with nothing to slow them,
crumpled into snow and ground,
split through, a dark season,
frosty without you.

3:05
No sight of you
in my dreams, the
door that won't latch
creaks to and fro with
the brisk air,
keeping you at bay
in that silver corner.

3:15
Seriously now, we all
must sleep one day,
and here I lie naked,
drawn and quartered,
giving myself to your absence.
The land is cold, but
my room is colder still.

3:30
You're in another town,
a distance I can't match,
spirit to spirit in grey,
in white, this skin

I sometimes share with you,
eyes flickering like icicles,
nipping at the windows.

An arctic season,
days of silent nights.

When it ends, it ends,
and I will be 25.

Because You Didn't Want To Hurt Me

Okay,
Maybe you were right.
I've got a bone to pick,
but not one you can see:

underneath the fog,
deep within the crook
of my termite-eaten tree,
hides that secret summer.

I dwell on the past;
yes, I admit it.
I keep you there
because it's the only
place I can be with
you now.

I have not forgotten:

how you told me once that
I was the person you
wanted to stay
furthest away from,

because I was the
one you loved the most.

In Extremis

Five years dwelling
six feet deep,
and the sound of
the tap dripping,
a west-side
water torture,
is the only way out.

I want another pill,
another shot,
a shovel to pack
me in or get me out.

I want you
the way we were,
pressed inside each
other like the
stale breath of coffins.

Five years hung up
on the tears
that wet your stained
sheets, and all
you can offer
now is a
glazed glance backward.

Lust

On Wednesday
the locusts feed
off the wisdom
in my eyes,

gorge themselves
on the pale
reflection of you
engraved in
that murky stillness.

If they could
taste the bitter
fruit in my heart,
they wouldn't
stay so long.

If they could
burrow into
what's left of
myself, they
would know that
I make an
awful hiding place.

Scorpio (2003)

the poison still drips,

and just when it seems
there's nothing left
to hurt, the
spider bites again.

Communion

You've got that carrion smile
dripping off your face
like you're still hungry.

My web isn't enough for you,
my tendrils can't hold you for long,

twitching,
snarling,
tearing at my alabaster skin
until the final wound wraps
you up to your throat,

until you can't scream anymore.

I Heard You The First Time

There's something
endearing about
those now-mauve
scars, little
marks like fallen
eyelashes, only
in the wrong place.

From teeth or nails?
Rope or wire?
Like tiny brushstrokes
on an odd canvas.
By hunger or despair?
Love or spite?

You think I
wasn't listening,

but I was just
admiring my
handiwork.

Tableau

The glass that
shattered against the wall,
the curtains torn to shreds,
the furniture upturned,
the paintings smashed in half,
your blood-smeared face
peering from the corner.

Anniversary

I can cut deeper
than any lie she's
used on you.

My fingers can slip
around your throat
before you have the
chance to whisper
my name,
can tighten like
leather bands when
you gasp you love me.

Don't think I
don't know what
crawls around in
your brain when
you're inside me.

Don't think I
don't know what
eats you alive when
you're away from me.

I am the one
who planted
the seed,
the one who pulled
the strings taut
across your heart,

the one who

won't fucking
let go.

The Stain Reveals The Real Intention

It spreads from your navel
like a spider web,
faint pink at first
until you gaze intently at it
and see the interconnected
capillaries rising to the surface,
pulsing red with fresh blood.

Then in a few days it
changes tint, tanning.
Like ringworm, you say,
your mouth full of my
flesh. *Or your nipples
when you were pregnant.*
And you run your finger
around one to prove your
point. I sigh.

Still it spreads further,
a warm blush enveloping
your body. It's like a
pall, or an accident with
fire. I lick my lips:

The distinguishing mark of prey.

Just Say It Already

Not one for
dancing around
the point,
love.

I've waited over
a decade for
your answer,

chewed through
bone and sinew
to arrive at the
heart
of the matter,

losing teeth,
gums bled dry,

to find nothing but
rust and that same old
metal taste again.

Determined

I've survived
my death
fifteen times
over now.

Each round
was just as raw,
just as unbridled,
but easier than the last.

*(I'm really just
stating the obvious
because you're
slow, and I like
the way it makes
my voice sound.)*

Honestly,
you should
know nothing
that stubborn
ends.

But, go on, then.

Give it another shot.

www.ingramcontent.com/pod-product-compliance
Lightning Source LLC
Chambersburg PA
CBHW021219020426
42331CB00003B/381